CARDINAL
SPELLMAN
THE MAN

CARDINAL SPELLMAN
THE MAN

by Warren Steibel

With an Introduction by
Francis Cardinal Spellman

Appleton-Century
New York

Photographs by Dan McCoy

APPLETON-CENTURY
AFFILIATE OF
MEREDITH PRESS | First edition

Library of Congress Catalog Card Number: 66-27903

Manufactured in the United States of America for Meredith Press

CARDINAL
SPELLMAN
THE MAN

Introduction

Fifty years is a long time. Many things happen, much to be remembered and much forgotten. When Mr. Steibel came to me to ask if he might prepare a television program and this book, entitled "Cardinal Spellman: The Man," I had mixed feelings. It did not seem to me that my memories would be of interest to more than a few persons — to my family, to some of my colleagues, and to some old friends. And I remembered what Cardinal Gasparri told me when he was asked to collect his memoirs. He declined, saying: "The interesting things I cannot tell, and the things which I can tell are not interesting." But Mr. Steibel insisted that a number of people would be interested in the people and the values that helped shape my life, and that my story could be a source of encouragement for young people now who are trying to build lives of dignity and purpose.

Naturally I have been pleased by the good reception the television program seems to have received. It certainly was an unusual experience for me to have cameras filming motion pictures, a photographer taking still pictures (for this book), and sound equipment recording my words as I traveled about here in New York and when I returned to Whitman, Massachusetts, where I was born. It was a moving experience to revisit places filled with memories of my childhood, and to take time for reminiscences and recollections with my brothers and sisters and their families.

Perhaps the most poignant memories occasioned during the making of the show were those brought back so vividly when one day Mr. Steibel came with newsreels taken years ago on visits to various battle-fronts. I have always felt that my most satisfying moments as a priest have been spent with those who serve our country so selflessly in the Armed Forces.

I should like to express my gratitude to Mr. Steibel and to Ted Purdy of Meredith Press for the care they have taken in preparing this little book, and to Dan McCoy for his excellent work on the photography.

The book has given me pleasure, and I hope that others may find in it some measure of enjoyment.

✠ F. Cardinal Spellman

✠ Francis Cardinal Spellman

ST. PATRICK'S DAY PARADE

St. Patrick's Day Parade. Always a great day for the Irish — and always a great day for His Eminence, Francis Cardinal Spellman, as he greets the marchers from the steps of St. Patrick's Cathedral. To the marchers and Americans everywhere, his familiar face is a living symbol of the strong faith and power of the Roman Catholic Church. For the remainder of the 585 million Roman Catholics of the world, he is almost equally well-known as the Pope's envoy and the most traveled Roman Catholic since Marco Polo.

Respected and revered, and yet to many too little known except as a great prelate. But what of the man beneath the Cardinal's miter? The man of seventy-seven now celebrating his fiftieth year as a priest?

Where does he come from? What is he like? Isn't there something about this man and his story that is typically American — American at its best — an almost Horatio Alger tale of a boy born in a small New England town before the turn of the century who rose to great prominence and renown?

With his consent, we wish to present, with pictures and his own words and the words of his friends, an intimate portrait of a warm and kind human being — Cardinal Spellman, the Man.

THE
CARDINAL
AT
HOME

The residence of the Archbishop of New York is an imposing five-story mansion of Gothic design nestled back of St. Patrick's Cathedral at 452 Madison Avenue. It was built in 1882 from plans by the architect of the Cathedral, Edward Renwick, who also built Grace Church on Broadway.

The Cardinal spends most of his day in this building, since it serves both as office and as home. Living here with him are his two associates and close friends, Bishop Terence Cook and Monsignor Patrick V. Ahern, P.A.

Downstairs there are several opulent Victorian reception and living rooms and a dining room; on the second floor are the offices and a small private apartment which comprises the Cardinal's living quarters; on the third is his private chapel.

On a recent evening Robert Considine, an old friend, came to interview the Cardinal at his residence. It was shortly before His Eminence celebrated the fiftieth anniversary of his ordination as a priest. Monsignor Ahern greeted him and took him through the first-floor rooms, before Considine went upstairs to see the Cardinal.

THE LIVING ROOM

CONSIDINE. It's good to be back in this famous old mansion again. With all the office buildings being built left and right around here, I guess this is one of the last homes remaining on Madison Avenue.

AHERN. Yes, and it remains completely unchanged from what it was when Cardinal Spellman first came here in 1939. Everything is just the same except the new curtains.

CONSIDINE. You don't see lace curtains like these much these days.

AHERN. Everybody admires them, especially the ladies.

CONSIDINE. And the "lace curtain Irish," no doubt.

AHERN. This front parlor is where His Eminence normally receives visitors. Anybody coming to call on him would be received in here.

CONSIDINE (*pointing to a portrait*). Is that his predecessor, Cardinal Hayes?

AHERN. Cardinal Hayes is over here.

CONSIDINE. Who was the first cardinal to live in the house?

AHERN. Cardinal McCluskey. We have this bust of him. He was the first American cardinal to receive the red hat at old St. Patrick's on Mulberry Street, way back in 1875.

THE THRONE ROOM

AHERN. This is the throne room or the second parlor. We don't use this very much, except, for instance, when people come to make a presentation formally to the Cardinal. We take group pictures in here, because this is a very nice background.

CONSIDINE. And what's this? It looks like a jukebox.

AHERN. Actually, it is. It was made especially for the Cardinal. You can see it has his coat of arms on it. And it can play records for thirty-seven and a half hours. We use it for music sometimes during luncheon or dinner to brighten things up.

CONSIDINE. What does the Cardinal like in music?

AHERN. Well, he likes all sorts of music. But we always kid him and say his favorite song is "Danny Boy," and then I always have to sing it.

CONSIDINE. How about liturgical music? Does he mix it in with popular?

AHERN. Well, we don't have any liturgical music on this. It's just dinner music or for luncheon when we have guests. This, of course, is a photograph taken with John the Twenty-third.

CONSIDINE. They were great friends?

AHERN. Yes, they were, they were.

CONSIDINE. It was through Pope John that millions were able to see Michelangelo's "Pietà" at the World's Fair.

AHERN. That's right. I believe as many as twenty-seven million actually did see it. And it came about in such a casual way. Cardinal Spellman was asked by His Holiness to have a Vatican Pavilion at the Fair, and His Holiness offered the Pietà as the outstanding work of art he could send for it. But the Holy Father died before the Fair opened, and then Pope Paul VI kept the bargain — and it was a tremendous success, the biggest single attraction.

CONSIDINE. Is this where Pope Paul VI sat when he was here?

AHERN. That's right. He came, as everybody knows, on the fourth of October last. But this is not the chair he actually sat in; it's the one in back of it. That chair is always left facing the picture of the Holy Father, and it's there only for his use. Nobody else uses it. They have the same setup in the house of every cardinal, in case the Pope should come along to visit.

CONSIDINE. You mean every cardinal has a chair waiting for the Pope to show up?

AHERN. Yes, but it doesn't happen too frequently. He surprised everybody when he came to New York.

CONSIDINE. It certainly was a great day.

THE DINING ROOM

AHERN. Here we have the dining room.

CONSIDINE. Who comes to lunch with the Cardinal?

AHERN. Oh, just about everybody; I'd say we have guests nearly every day in the year — just informal luncheons, friends and people who know the Cardinal.

CONSIDINE. He never goes out to restaurants, does he?

AHERN. No. It is practically a principle with him that he doesn't go out for anything except public dinners. Normally he eats here. Breakfast, of course, alone, after he says Mass. And there would be just His Eminence, Bishop Cook, and myself, and the same for supper. We usually don't have any guests in the evening.

CONSIDINE. Is this where he entertained the Pope when he was here?

AHERN. This is where our Holy Father had his lunch. He sat there, and His Eminence there. Monsignor Macchi, the secretary of the Holy Father, was the only other one with them.

CONSIDINE *(looking at portrait)*. Who is this, now?

AHERN. This is Archbishop Hughes, Bob. He was the first Archbishop of New York, back around the time of the Civil War.

CONSIDINE. He was a friend of Lincoln's, I recall.

AHERN. Yes, he was.

CONSIDINE. Lincoln asked him to do something about the draft riots here in town.

AHERN. Yes, he had a very eventful reign.

THE CARDINAL CHATS WITH
BOB CONSIDINE

CONSIDINE. Your Eminence, lots of people going past your residence must wonder what it's like behind the lace curtains, and this is a great opportunity, particularly in this time of ecumenism, to let the world see how a prince of the Church lives and to learn more about him.

CARDINAL SPELLMAN. Well, I have nothing to hide.

CONSIDINE. When did you get the call? Was there a special hour or day or moment when you determined to become a priest?

CARDINAL SPELLMAN. No. I had thought about it for a long time. And, finally, on graduation day at Fordham, my mother and father came over, and I told them I would like to stay and become a priest — I would like to try. And my father said, "Whatever you want, but be as good as you can at it, and your mother and I will support you in your work." And they were willing that I should go to Rome, because they wanted me to make a complete break from Massachusetts. I was away from home for five years, and I didn't see any one of my relatives at all. Nowadays, boys who go to Rome have their parents at their ordination and things like that. I was never able to do that.

CONSIDINE. You had to study Italian as well as Latin, I suppose?

CARDINAL SPELLMAN. Yes, but you learn it anyway when you're living in the country.

CONSIDINE. Yes. And when you came back to Boston, you went into newspaper work briefly, did you not? Weren't you on *The Pilot?*

CARDINAL SPELLMAN. Not right away. I was appointed a curate in All Saints' Parish in Roxbury, and it was a most happy experience. The pastor was very kind and very helpful, and the first curate was wonderful to me. So, I led a happy life, visiting the sick and doing all the things that a curate does in a parish. I had charge of a Sunday school and was in charge of the confirmation classes. Yes, it was a very wonderful life.

1916 — a priest at All Saints' Church, Roxbury, Massachusetts.

CONSIDINE. A curate's life can be just as rewarding as the life of a prince of the Church in many ways, I suppose.

CARDINAL SPELLMAN. Yes it's the same thing. In fact, the other is better. Here, I have to busy myself, while, as a curate, others kept me busy.

Francis Spellman, a member of the Class of 1916 of the North American College in Rome.

"I WANTED TO BE A CHAPLAIN"

CARDINAL SPELLMAN. When the war broke out, the first World War, I wanted to be a chaplain, and Cardinal O'Connell gave me permission. So I volunteered. At that time, the Cardinal told you what service you should try for, and I was told to try for the Navy. You had to go to Washington for a physical examination. So I went, and another priest and I — a classmate of mine in Rome — had our examinations together, and he was perfect. I was found to be a quarter of an inch too short.

CONSIDINE. For the Navy?

CARDINAL SPELLMAN. For the Navy.

CONSIDINE. Sounds like a basketball team, instead of fighting a war.

CARDINAL SPELLMAN. Well, I wasn't supposed to fight. I was a chaplain. Surgeon General Blue was head of the Navy, and he waived that physical defect of a quarter of an inch too short. And then I thought it was all settled, but then there was a mental examination. And I didn't do too well in that.

CONSIDINE. Oh, come on — really.

CARDINAL SPELLMAN. No, because that was before the ecumenical movement, and the head chaplain didn't treat me very nicely. He didn't think I was obsequious enough to be a chaplain, or something. At any rate, he dismissed me.

I thought I had passed, because Surgeon General Blue had told me that I would be accepted and would receive my commission in a short time. So I went back to Boston and waited. And I didn't hear anything. And like most everybody when he gets into trouble, I went to my congressman. My congressman was George Tinkham. And he found out very quickly what the trouble was — the head of the chaplains had rejected me as temperamentally unfit to be a chaplain in the Navy.

So I went back to Cardinal O'Connell and asked if I could apply for the Army. And since no one is supposed to incriminate himself, I told the Cardinal that I was a quarter of an inch too short to be a Naval chaplain, and could I try for the Army? He gave me permission, and I went down to Fort Banks in Boston Harbor for an examination. I was called up, and my disposition was said to be lovely and sweet, and so I was accepted as an Army chaplain.

But in the meantime, I had bought the Navy uniform, and when I found out I couldn't get into the Navy, I went back to the store and said, "I made a mistake. I am in the Army instead of the Navy." I found the turnover value of a naval uniform of a chaplain a quarter of an inch too short is very, very little.

I went back to Cardinal O'Connell — there were twelve of us who were going to be chaplains — and the Cardinal gave us a talk on how to be a chaplain. He hadn't been one himself, but he had a general idea of what a chaplain should do. And we all listened, and we paid attention, and he looked at me, and he said, "Did you understand everything I said?" At that time, I had a good memory, so I said I did. In the meantime, I had gotten better acquainted with the Cardinal. We all started to go out, and he said he wanted to see me. He said, "You go into the other room and write down everything I said." So, I wrote it down. I wrote down everything he said and a couple of things I thought he should have said.

CONSIDINE. What he should have said?

CARDINAL SPELLMAN. What he could have said, anyway. And I brought it back to him, and he said, "I am notifying you that I am withdrawing your ecclesiastical endorsement." And I said, "What does that mean?" And he said, "It means that you are out of the Army. You are appointed to the staff of *The Pilot*. The circulation has gone down, and you are to promote subscriptions." So, that's the story of my military experience.

CONSIDINE. Well, when you look back on it, Your Eminence, and that you later became Military Vicar, it's hard to believe. You have something in common with General Eisenhower. He tried to get into the Naval Academy and was terribly distressed when he was turned down for some piddling thing like that.

CARDINAL SPELLMAN. He didn't buy his uniforms, though.

CONSIDINE. He probably got your old uniform.

For — His Eminence Francis Cardinal Spellman with the deep regard of his old and devoted friend —

Dwight Eisenhower

21

In Venice in 1927 with former teacher.

ITALY, 1925–1932

CONSIDINE. And then you went back to Rome?

CARDINAL SPELLMAN. In 1925, we had a pilgrimage. And the pilgrimage ahead of us was from Rochester and Buffalo. Nobody in the group knew Italian. And the Pope, Pius the Eleventh, wanted a translation made of what he said. I was in the next group, and they asked if anybody knew Italian in that group — in our group. I said I did. So the Holy Father gave his little talk, and then he beckoned to me to translate. This time, I put in a few things the Pope might have said.

CONSIDINE. Was that your first meeting with Pius the Eleventh?

CARDINAL SPELLMAN. That was the first time I had any contact like that with him. He seemed pleased and thanked me, and I thanked him. At that time, they discovered they needed somebody to assist the Papal Secretary of State. So I was recommended by some of the professors I had studied under in Rome, and I was asked if I would like to come to Rome. I said I would. So I was appointed for a year, on trial, in the Secretary of Sate's office — that was then Cardinal Gasparri.

CONSIDINE. What were your duties?

CARDINAL SPELLMAN. I translated not only the letters, but also for people who had been granted an audience with the Holy Father. I would be admitted to the audience with them. I would translate and write. And then, in addition, the Knights of Columbus had opened playgrounds in Rome but were unable to get them organized, so I helped with that. And I remained in Italy, instead of one year, seven years — until 1932.

CONSIDINE. Was it then that you helped dedicate, with Marconi and Pius the Eleventh, the Vatican radio, which at that time, I believe, was the most powerful radio in the world?

CARDINAL SPELLMAN. It was 1931, and I took only a minor part. I translated what the Holy Father had to say into English, but it happened to be the first worldwide broadcast, so I was very happy and pleased to be honored by being selected to talk for him. At that time, I had never heard of radio broadcasts, and I had no idea of the impression that radio broadcasts made on people. I was amazed later on when I was identified as being the one who had translated the Holy Father's words.

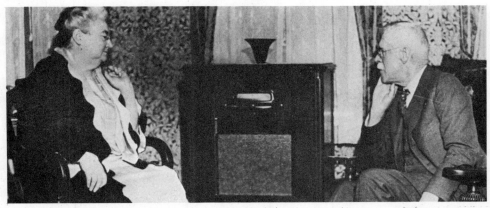

Cardinal Spellman's parents, William and Ellen Spellman, listen proudly over their radio in Whitman to their son's English translation of the Pope's message.

Boston Post, July 5, 1931.

ITALY AND POPE NEAR RUPTURE

Mussolini Resents Manner of Giving Out Vatican Note---Mgr. Spellman the Pope's Courier

Mgr. Spellman as Pope's Encyclical Messenger

ROME, July 4—It was reported tonight that the Vatican messenger who took the Pope's encyclical to Paris to be published throughout the world was Mgr. Francis J. Spellman, whose home is in Whitman, Mass.

Mgr. Spellman is an accomplished Latin scholar as it was he who spoke the English version of the Pope's broadcasts made this year by Pope Pius from the Vatican's wireless station.

ROME, July 4 (AP)—Possibility of the withdrawal of the Papal Nuncio at Rome was a subject of discussion by diplomatic observers tonight as a result of the widening of the breach between the church and state by the encyclical of Pope Pius XI on Fascism.

Nothing approaching a diplomatic rupture was foreseen, but observers believed the Vatican might withdraw its Nuncio as a gesture of indignation to emphasize the Pope's reiterated disapproval of Premier Mussolini's action against the Catholic clubs.

The government officially silent on the encyclical tonight, but it was evident it felt a resentment as much to the form of the document as to its manner.

The last Italian note to the Vatican protested against what it called the Pontiff's "trying his case" before world public opinion.

Regarding the Pontiff's contention that

MGR. FRANCIS J. SPELLMAN
Of Whitman, who is said to have carried the Pope's encyclical to the world.

the education of youth belongs to the church, the Fascist creed is an equally opposed to this that neither the government nor the Vatican authorities could see any real hope for a compromise.

This is the fundamental point that it has always been feared would become an issue, regardless of the peaceful settlement of the old relations between the Vatican and Rome which kept the Pope "prisoners" on papal territory.

Both Pope Pius and Premier Mussolini have a reputation for possessing firm wills, and since both insist upon the control of the education of youth it was believed in government circles that negotiations would offer little hope.

Method of Vatican Note Criticised

A great deal of Fascist criticism was being leveled at the Pontiff's method of publishing the encyclical. The fact that the document was published abroad, with a hint given here at Vatican City until it had almost reached the newspapers, was being construed as a reflection on the good faith of Fascism.

It was interpreted as meaning that Pope Pius believed Premier Mussolini might have prevented the transmission of the document, which was said by officials tonight to be "absurd."

The next move, it was conceded, is up to the government. The Vatican has demanded the reopening of the thousands of closed clubs. The government's reply, it was understood tonight, will probably be based on the Pope's encyclical. Both Premier Mussolini and Foreign Minister Grandi take the view that the encyclical renders further conversations extremely difficult.

The belief prevailed that if the Pontiff should decide to withdraw the papal nuncio he would leave a charge d'affaires as the medium of further contacts.

Neither side, it was believed, considers that there has been a complete rupture or nullification of all of the work accomplished by the Lateran treaty.

Boston Globe, July 12, 1931.

MONSIGNOR SPELLMAN, "THE NERVY KID FROM WHITMAN," WHO FLEW FROM ROME TO PARIS WITH POPE'S MESSAGE TO ESCAPE CENSORSHIP

Today He Is Secret Chamberlain to His Holiness Pius XI, Who Played Role in Pope's First Broadcast to World and Made Dramatic Flight Over Fascist Lines— But Massachusetts Town Remembers "Frank" Spellman as Shortstop on High School Nine and a Youngster Who Wasn't Afraid to Use His Fists on Occasion

By LOUIS M. LYONS

HAD any courier's deed since the taking of the message to Garcia so appealed to the imagination as that flight which carried the Pope's defiant answer to Mussolini from Rome to Paris, beyond the reach of Fascist suppression?

That the deed went unheralded at the time and has yet been intimated only in veiled paragraphs from Rome but adds to the romance of the circumstances which caused a young American priest of the Vatican to be sent secretly by airplane across the Alps to give a Papal encyclical to the world.

The encyclical was dated June 19. It reached the press of the world on the 4th of July. There is a mysterious gap in these intervening days that gives dramatic meaning to that ancient title—secret chamberlain to the Pope—which is the title borne by Mgr Francis J. Spellman.

Former Whitman Boy Courier

It takes nothing from the drama of the event that the courier-prelate was 15 years ago a round-faced boy in the town of Whitman. His distinctions then among his peers were chiefly related to the game he played at shortstop, and to the way he handled his fists in the boxing bouts that his playmates enjoyed in his father's barn.

"Frank Spellman was always a nervy kid" was the comment of the Whitman druggist who played on the High School baseball team when Mgr Spellman was captain.

"Last Sunday night 'is a big white house behind a row of Elm maples. Mrs William Spellman sat with her two sons and their wives and her two daughters and their husbands and her grandchildren gathered about her, as they always are on Sunday evenings.

The telephone rang. "Transatlantic operator." Then she heard across the Atlantic the voice of her eldest son, Mgr Spellman, speaking from Rome. He knew that the news of his part in the release of the encyclical from Paris had leaked out. He wanted to assure his mother that he was safe

after the flight, and well. The next day's newspapers carried an Associated Press dispatch which named Mgr Spellman as the flying courier of the Pope.

It was not the first thrill of pride and wonder that had come winging across the Atlantic to Mrs Spellman this year.

In the same room with her children and grandchildren about her, she had heard her son's voice tell that of the Pope in the first radio broadcast from the Vatican. He not only transmitted the Pope's words, but he also translated them for the ears of all English-speaking listeners.

A month later she heard his voice again transmitting another translation of the Pope's—the encyclical on labor.

Through the swift succession of honors that have come to him in Rome in the years, Mgr Spellman has never forgotten his native town. Every dispatch relating to his career places him as "of Whitman, Mass."

The forbears of the Plymouth County priest go back some 200 years in offical expression of acknowledgment of this recognition he has been so careful to secure for the home of his happy childhood.

In Whitman, his father, William Spellman, was born and found business success among friendly townsfolk. His mother, Ellen M. Conway, was a native of Plympton, farther down in Plymouth County.

As a young man William Spellman

SPECIAL MISSION

CONSIDINE. Pius the Eleventh gave you a special mission. There have been so many Ian Fleming stories about that, haven't there? You flew out with Mussolini breathing heavily on your neck.

CARDINAL SPELLMAN. That's true. But I was given a message by the Holy Father to deliver because Mussolini was against us, and the Pope wanted it to be published outside of Italy.

CONSIDINE. It was about Catholic Youth Action?

CARDINAL SPELLMAN. Against Mussolini's action against the Catholic Youth groups. I took a train to Paris. I didn't fly out on a plane as some of the newspapers said, but I went in a train, and I stayed up all night translating the message into English. *Non Abbiamo Bisogno* — We Have No Need.

CONSIDINE. It was an encyclical, in effect, was it not?

CARDINAL SPELLMAN. Well, yes. So then I delivered it to all of the folks of the Associated Press and the United Press. We didn't have the UPI at that time, but I delivered it to every news agency. And then I tried to get back to Italy, but I was unable to do so, because my identity had been disclosed. And when I finally did get back to Italy, there were a lot of threats and cartoons in the papers against me.

One had me in an airplane scattering encyclicals, tearing down from the heavens the motto, "Peace on Earth to Men of Good Will" and putting up another slogan in its place, "Death on Earth to Men of Good Will." The second had a *blind* man coming to me and asking help. And I say to him, "For you — read this!" and I hand him an encyclical. Then the funniest of all was a man running up to me while I was passing out encyclicals like handbills on the street, and the man says to me, "Hurry up — come quick, there is a man dying!" And I answer, "Tell him to wait a few hours, because I have a few hundred more encyclicals to distribute!"

CONSIDINE. Did you ever see Mussolini? Did he ever say anything about it?

CARDINAL SPELLMAN. I knew him. But after I got back, I never saw him again.

CONSIDINE. There was a certain cooling in your relationship.

CARDINAL SPELLMAN. He made one mistake, and no one is allowed to make any mistakes. I mean, the idea of declaring war on the United States. I recall very well he called our chargé d'affaires and said, "My nation is at war with the United States." And our chargé d'affaires said, "Those are the saddest words that I have ever heard, and Italy will regret them." And, of course, Italy did regret them.

CARDINAL PACELLI (POPE PIUS XII)

CARDINAL SPELLMAN. I knew Pius the Twelfth the best of the Popes, because I was in the office when Cardinal Pacelli was made Secretary of State in 1930, when Cardinal Gasparri became ill.

CONSIDINE. Did you accompany Cardinal Pacelli from Rome on his famous visit to America?

CARDINAL SPELLMAN. No. That was in 1936, and I had come back to America four years before that, when I was made Bishop of Boston. I was parish priest in Newton Center, Massachusetts, and auxiliary to Cardinal O'Connell. But I met him when he arrived here in New York.

CONSIDINE. He made a great hit, a great impression on a lot of people at that time. He had a great mind, according to everybody who came in contact with him. He seemed to have a universality about him in the way he met people; he had something to say to everybody. He was, in effect, the start of ecumenism in many ways, because so many people of different faiths came back speaking so highly of him, how nice he had been; and he spoke to them usually in their own language — he could speak six or eight languages.

Mrs. Nicholas Brady kisses the episcopal ring of Cardinal Pacelli as Cardinal Spellman and onlookers greet the Secretary of State. Mrs. Brady was the widow of Nicholas F. Brady who acted as hostess at her Long Island estate, Inisfada (Gaelic for "Long Island"), for Cardinal Pacelli, who used it as his American headquarters. Later, this estate was given to the Church.

27

Inisfada

CARDINAL SPELLMAN. Oh, yes, he was a linguist, and he was a great man. He saw all of America, in the month he was here, from New York to San Francisco. And I remember when I asked the pilot of the plane how was the visibility at the Grand Canyon, he said, "It is clear," and we made a little detour of a few hundred miles so that Cardinal Pacelli could see this great natural wonder of our country. And it was the same at Niagara Falls.

A visit to Mount Vernon.

ELEVATION

CONSIDINE. When did you know that you were to become a cardinal? How is one told? Did you get a "greetings" postcard like going into the Army?

CARDINAL SPELLMAN. No, sort of an airmail special. Actually, I was told by the Apostolic Delegate via telegram that I would be a cardinal. That was in 1946, just twenty years ago.

CONSIDINE. What did you say?

CARDINAL SPELLMAN. Thank you.

CONSIDINE. You flew to Rome when it was not considered particularly safe to fly over at that time. I recall seeing you off at the airport. It was a great time.

CARDINAL SPELLMAN. It was the first transatlantic flight of a TWA Constellation. We had two chartered planes — *The Star of Rome* and *The Colosseum*. The red hat which was given to me by the Pope was the same one that had been given to Pius the Twelfth when he was made cardinal. And then he put it aside, and some years afterward he took it and gave it to me. That's why I consider it very precious, because it belonged to Pope Pius the Twelfth. And I hope that it won't have to go along with the other cardinals' hats up in the Cathedral, after I die. That's the custom. When the cardinal dies, they hoist his hat up to the roof of the Cathedral until it disintegrates. So, I bought a case and put it under glass in the Gold Room of the chancery, and I hope that my successor will keep it there.

Pope Pius bestows red hat upon Cardinal Spellman in Vatican City, Rome. The Cardinal is kneeling before the throne of Pope Pius XII in the Basilica of St. Peter's as the Pontiff intones a prayer before bestowing the red hat, during the final rites in his elevation.

MILITARY VICAR

CONSIDINE. What was your first mission as military vicar?

CARDINAL SPELLMAN. It was in the summer of 1942 when I went to visit the soldiers and chaplains in the Aleutians, to Dutch Harbor, Prince George, Fort St. John, White-horse, Fairbanks, Galena, Nome, Anchorage, Kodiak, Cold Bay, Unalaska, and Annette Island. That was two weeks, and we traveled eighteen thousand miles, and on the way back I visited every camp coming down the West Coast — the training camps in those days. And the next year, when we started to have the Expeditionary Force in Europe, I went with them over there and was in North Africa. I left in February and was away almost six months. The trip covered, according to the news-papers, forty-six thousand miles from New York to Portugal, Spain, Vatican City, Gibraltar, French Morocco, Algeria, England, Ireland, Scotland, Libya, Malta, Tunisia, Egypt, Palestine, Transjordan, Syria, Lebanon, Turkey, Iraq, Iran, Eritrea, Ethiopia, Anglo-Egyptian Sudan, Uganda, Kenya, Tanganyika, Madagascar, Mau-ritius, Mozambique, Union of South Africa, Belgian Congo, Rhodesia, French Equa-torial Africa, Nigeria, Gold Coast, Ascension Island, Brazil, British Guiana, Puerto Rico, and back to New York. It was under wartime conditions, but the worst was North Africa which was very hard, and Rommel was being very difficult. Our armies had a lot of casualties, and our men had to fight very hard with great sacrifices.

CONSIDINE. A lot of people who don't know Your Eminence ask me, "Why does he travel like this? Why doesn't he stay home and relax? The man is seventy!"

CARDINAL SPELLMAN *(interrupting). Seventy!* Thank you very much. Seventy-seven.

CONSIDINE. Well, this is a special dispensation from the laity. Last Christmas, espe-cially, it seemed so bleak and lonely, but not to you — you don't feel that way. You don't miss the hearth at home at Christmas.

CARDINAL SPELLMAN. I meet more of my fellow Americans across the ocean than I get to meet here in New York. But Vietnam wasn't my hardest trip. My hardest trip was to the South Pole. That was two Christmases ago. I was two years younger. But I didn't know that I would be able to go that time, because I hadn't been feeling well, and I had advice that I shouldn't go, but I thought to myself how unfortunate it would be if I didn't go, so that was the motive.

CONSIDINE. Is there any place in the world you haven't been or wish to go?

CARDINAL SPELLMAN. No, I have been every place I wish to go, and there were a few I didn't care about going to.

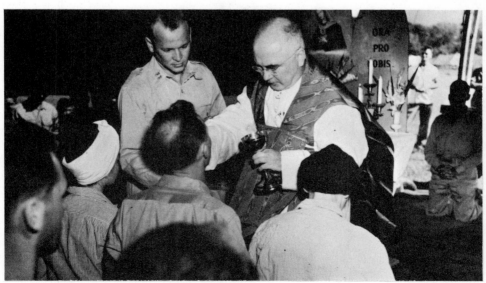

THE POPE'S VISIT

Considine. I know you had so much to do with Pope Paul's visit and arranging that great day.

Cardinal Spellman. Yes. October fourth.

Considine. Do you think he will continue his travels, having set this amazing precedent?

Cardinal Spellman. Well, he seems to enjoy traveling, and I am sure he does a lot of good by traveling. He sees a lot of people and talks to a lot of people and says a lot of inspiring things, so I hope he will continue.

Considine. That day was — in my mind as an ordinary layman — the greatest day the Church ever had in this country.

Cardinal Spellman. No question about that. It was a tremendous experience when he was received with such respect, such deference, such reverence; and his message was really a plea to the leaders of the world to have peace.

Considine. Thank you so much.

Cardinal Spellman. Thank you, Bob. Thank you very much.

The desk in the study

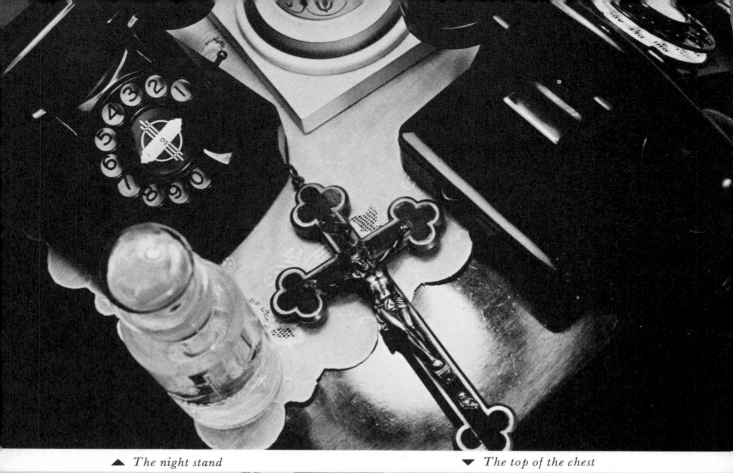

▲ *The night stand*   ▼ *The top of the chest*

▲ *A picture above the bed*

▼ *His bureau*

HOMECOMING

"Whitman — My Mother Town," is the name of a poem written by Francis Cardinal Spellman, penned out of a lifelong love for the small New England town which was his childhood home:

> *Whitman, my mother town,*
> *Dear to my soul are the scenes of thy keeping;*
> *Beneath thy sod my kinsfolk sleep,*
> *Their eyes turned starward;*
> *And I dream the dreams of long ago.*
> *I, a priest of God, son of this soil of America,*
> *Whitman, my mother town!*

It was in Whitman that Francis Spellman, son of William and Ellen Spellman, was born on May 4, 1889. And it was in Whitman that young Frank Spellman was to grow up in a setting and environment typical of many an American town. Approximately

twenty miles southwest of Boston, Whitman at the turn of the century was a happy place for a boy — gathering hay, taking care of the horses, raking the leaves, fetching water. And those happy childhood memories have never been forgotten as the Cardinal has returned in trip after trip to Whitman during the intervening years.

But in all the many times the Cardinal has returned to Whitman, he has never gone back to the beautiful white frame building of Georgian design at 96 Beulah Street — the house which contains so many of his childhood memories.

When the Cardinal decided to go back to the house, accompanied by his niece, Mrs. Frances McCarthy, it turned out that it was approximately forty-five years since he had been to this, his boyhood home.

Mrs. Holmes, the present owner of 96 Beulah Street, graciously took the Cardinal and his niece through this emotional revisiting of the old home.

RETURN TO THE BOYHOOD HOME

Cardinal Spellman and his niece, Mrs. Frances McCarthy, approach the house.

FRANCES. Oh, it's wonderful to come back here.

CARDINAL SPELLMAN. This is a tulip tree. And a magnolia tree in the distance.

FRANCES. Where was the tennis court? Didn't you and Uncle Martin build a tennis court?

CARDINAL SPELLMAN. Out there, yes.

FRANCES. All by yourselves?

CARDINAL SPELLMAN. After the trees blew down in a storm in 1898.

FRANCES. Is this the original door?

CARDINAL SPELLMAN. I don't remember.

(They knock on the door. Mrs. Holmes opens it and invites them in.)

MRS. HOLMES. Good morning, Cardinal Spellman. Welcome, welcome home.

CARDINAL SPELLMAN. Hello, Mrs. Holmes. How are you? Thank you, thank you very much. Do you know my niece?

MRS. HOLMES. I do. Will you go in?

CARDINAL SPELLMAN. Thank you very much.

Mrs. Holmes. We'll go in the living room, sir. To the right.

Cardinal Spellman. You've changed the stairs here.

Mrs. Holmes. Yes, I think you'll find a lot of changes. But I hope it's home.

Cardinal Spellman. Oh, it is. A home full of memories.

Mrs. Holmes. Yes, and nice ones. Wonderful.

Cardinal Spellman. May I take off my coat?

Mrs. Holmes. Yes, do. You'll be more comfortable. I'm sorry I didn't think of it.

Cardinal Spellman. Oh, you can't think of everything.

Mrs. Holmes. Come over by the fire. Now, does it look the same to you?

Cardinal Spellman. Well, I remember when we came here, this was a bare room when my father bought the place. A big room and bare, and no furniture. It wasn't furnished until I came back from Rome after my ordination in the priesthood, and my parents fixed up the room so we could have a little reception. So that's when it was furnished for the first time. And then as children, of course, we played here in this room. And the fireplace was in the other room. Because I can remember, see — I'm ten years older than my youngest brother. We were five of us. And at Christmas we hung our stockings. Even though we still didn't believe in Santa Claus, we pretended we did believe in him. So, then, we'd come down when the presents would be arranged, and we'd take a preview before we were supposed to see them in the morning — Christmas morning. Well, it's — as I say — it's filled with memories, happy ones. And I'm so grateful that you allowed me to come and see it again.

MRS. HOLMES. We still look out on the back lawns and gardens. You had a lovely orchard, I know.

CARDINAL SPELLMAN. Yes, yes, a beautiful orchard.

Mrs. Holmes. We still have apple trees . . . and pears . . .

Cardinal Spellman. Seckel pears and Bartlett pears . . .

Mrs. Holmes. Yes, they're still here.

Cardinal Spellman. And red Astrachan apples . . .

Mrs. Holmes. Those are gone.

Cardinal Spellman. Well, we won't weep about it.

Mrs. Holmes. No, we won't weep over apples. I presume it has changed in other ways.

Cardinal Spellman. Yes. We had the whole square when my father bought it. And then, as each one of us went off to school, he sold house lots, so he could pay our tuition.

Mrs. Holmes. Well, that's been done before.

Frances. I'd like to see the bedroom that you had when you were here.

Cardinal Spellman. Well, they moved me around two or three times, but I can find all three.

Mrs. Holmes. Well, now, we aren't using the entire second floor. Perhaps we won't find your bedroom.

Cardinal Spellman. Oh, I'm sure it's up there. Shall I go first?

Mrs. Holmes. Yes, you go first.

Cardinal Spellman. This staircase is new, too.

Mrs. Holmes. Yes, I think they've changed the stairway. I think it's remarkable that you remember all these details.

Frances. Which was the room where you used to study?

Cardinal Spellman. Well, thank you for saying "study."

Mrs. Holmes. Well, you must have.

Cardinal Spellman. Well, I didn't do much in high school. This was my mother's parlor.

FRANCES. I'd like to have my sister see it sometime. We've heard stories about this house all our lives, you know, Mrs. Holmes.

MRS. HOLMES. That would be fine. You'll come again, won't you?

CARDINAL SPELLMAN. I'd love to, Mrs. Holmes. It's been a great thrill for me.

MRS. HOLMES. It's been a pleasure.

FRANCES. Thanks, Mrs. Holmes. I hope I see you soon.

MRS. HOLMES. Good-bye, Frances.

A WALK

The Cardinal and his niece Frances leave the childhood home on Beulah Street and take a walk, passing by some of the places which were important while he was growing up.

CARDINAL SPELLMAN. This is the way I used to walk on my way to school.

FRANCES. So you've taken this walk a lot of times before.

CARDINAL SPELLMAN. Thousands of times. It's nice to see the trees are pretty much the same.

FRANCES. And the barn was right over there?

CARDINAL SPELLMAN. Yes. But it's been torn down now.

FRANCES. How many horses were there, three?

CARDINAL SPELLMAN. Two horses and a pony.

FRANCES. The pony was my mother's.

CARDINAL SPELLMAN. Well, we had several.

FRANCES. Oh, I only know about one. The horse was named "Daisy."

CARDINAL SPELLMAN. Then we had a pony when your mother came along. And she had another one.

FRANCES. Are all these houses just the same?

CARDINAL SPELLMAN. Oh, sure. Staples' and Betty Bowles', and this is where Harvey Danner lived, and that's Fred Douglas' house. I'm sorry to see the barn's gone — but there are no horses anymore.

FRANCES. And there was the well.

CARDINAL SPELLMAN. The well was right up there, back of that trellis.

FRANCES. They didn't have town water?

CARDINAL SPELLMAN. Well, we get it from Silver Lake now, but during my time, it was from Patrick Pond, which wasn't so good, they say.

FRANCES. The well was better and colder in the summertime.

CARDINAL SPELLMAN. Yes.

FRANCES. And these stone posts?

CARDINAL SPELLMAN. Those are new. In our time, we couldn't afford such luxuries.

THE DYER SCHOOL

FRANCES. See the Dyer School?

CARDINAL SPELLMAN. Yes, where I spent eight years. See, we had nine grades. And the fourth grade I went to Gurney School, but I was glad to come back to the Dyer School. And I had great memories, vivid memories, of all my teachers, and a very great, deep gratitude to them.

FRANCES. Did you start playing baseball when you were here at this school? Did they have a team?

CARDINAL SPELLMAN. Yes, well, we had a sort of a team — an altar boys' team. We had the baseball diamond out in back and Father Conan as our coach. And we came near beating Abington several times.

FRANCES. Only came near?

CARDINAL SPELLMAN. Yes. Well, they had a wonderful pitcher.

FRANCES. Who was that?

CARDINAL SPELLMAN. He became a priest. Father Donegan. And we didn't have as good a pitcher.

FRANCES. Who was *Whitman's* pitcher, for goodness' sake?

CARDINAL SPELLMAN. I was.

FRANCES. I thought you were shortstop.

CARDINAL SPELLMAN. Yes, at one time. We had, I think, eight boys in the school — no, we had enough to make it nine. The bottom story of the school was the first grade, and the ninth grade was up at the top.

FRANCES. And did you have a formal graduation ceremony?

CARDINAL SPELLMAN. Oh, sure. We got our diplomas. We didn't dress up in cap and gowns.

FRANCES. No?

CARDINAL SPELLMAN. Like they do nowadays. Well, it's wonderful to see it. We had our class pictures taken on those steps.

FRANCES. They still take them there.

HOLY GHOST CHURCH

CARDINAL SPELLMAN. Well, here we are at the Holy Ghost Church at Whitman.

FRANCES. Yes.

CARDINAL SPELLMAN. Well, it's wonderful to be back here where my mother and father were married and I was baptized and all the children were baptized; and where I served as altar boy and received my first Holy Communion and was confirmed and said my first Mass. So, I am pleased to come back and visit every time that I possibly can.

(Monsignor Frawley is in front of church.)

CARDINAL SPELLMAN. Good morning, Monsignor.

MONSIGNOR. Good morning, Cardinal. Welcome back.

CARDINAL SPELLMAN. It's good to see you. And my respects to the parish.

MONSIGNOR. Thank you very, very much. This has some very fond memories for you.

CARDINAL SPELLMAN. Yes, I was telling Frances, it was here my mother and father were married, and I was baptized, received my first Holy Communion, was confirmed, and celebrated my first Mass as a priest here in Whitman. After I was ordained in Rome and said my earlier Masses over there. And then, also, my parents were buried here and my grandparents, so, it's a very emotional experience to come back always.

MONSIGNOR. A lot of fond memories.

CARDINAL SPELLMAN. Yes, they are. Happy memories — and also, naturally, sad ones.

MONSIGNOR. We have a beautiful sanctuary downstairs that you gave in memory of your mother.

CARDINAL SPELLMAN. Yes.

FRANCES. Yes, it's a lovely altar.

CARDINAL SPELLMAN. Good-bye. Thank you very much.

MONSIGNOR. You're very welcome.

THE GROCERY STORE

FRANCES. There's the jewelry store, Uncle Frank, where the other store was.

CARDINAL SPELLMAN. I'm pleased that there's a store there, and I'm glad that we're finished with the grocery business. You know my father made us all work in the store.

FRANCES. That was a good idea, wasn't it?

CARDINAL SPELLMAN. It was an excellent idea. And I learned a lot from it. I remember, one day when I was trying to sell groceries, my father corrected me when I said to a customer, "Is that all?" He said, "Never say, 'Is that all?' Say, 'Is there anything else'?"

FRANCES. He finished the grocery business at the right time, I guess.

CARDINAL SPELLMAN. Yes, he did.

FRANCES. How many grocers were there in town, then?

CARDINAL SPELLMAN. Five. But they were all good-natured, no cutthroats.

FRANCES. And did Grandfather own these stores?

CARDINAL SPELLMAN. Yes. And sending children to school outside of Massachusetts lost all the stores. However, he was glad to pay for it. He was in the real-estate business as well.

FRANCES. Didn't you work on the streetcars as well as the grocery store?

CARDINAL SPELLMAN. Not in Whitman. It was the summer before I went to Rome for the North American College. I wanted to earn some money — more than my father would give me in the grocery store — so I went to work as a conductor on the Bay State Line. They had a car that ran from Grove Street in Boston to East Walpole. It was a very happy summer, but I remember once when I spent an extra dollar to get home an hour faster on the train, Papa warned me, "Don't do that again until your time is worth a dollar an hour — and I don't think it ever will be."

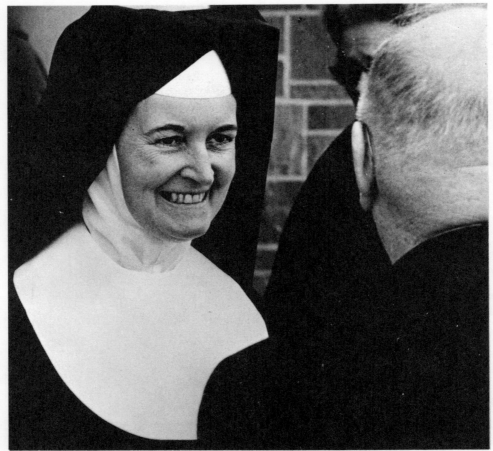

CARDINAL SPELLMAN HIGH SCHOOL

A stop to address his nephew Billy McCarthy's graduating class.

CARDINAL SPELLMAN. Good morning, everybody.

BILLY. It is my great pleasure to present today my uncle, Cardinal Spellman, the Archbishop of New York. We were hoping to have him for graduation, but since he cannot make it, we are most delighted to have him today.

CARDINAL SPELLMAN. Students of Cardinal Spellman High School, in Brockton, in Plymouth County, in the State of Massachusetts: I'm very happy to be here, and once more I express gratitude to Cardinal Cushing for honoring me by naming this wonderful high school. I am sorry I cannot be here for the graduation exercises. And I'm very sorry we lost to New Bedford High School, but we learn from defeats as well as from victories. I understand that you all do very well in class, which is more than I did when I was at Whitman High School. I didn't study hard enough, and I didn't have any Sisters to encourage me; but I had the lay teachers who were very wonderful — at least, they taught me how to spell, which is a great achievement these days.

CARDINAL SPELLMAN. I know that you are doing very well, and I'm glad to see the high school kept in such wonderful shape, because I notice that in these schools that are privately supported by religious and other groups the students are very careful in the maintenance of these buildings, and they realize that their fathers and mothers make great sacrifices for them so that they can have the advantages of high schools like this.

I know that you do appreciate all the sacrifices that are made for you, and by you, and by your parents, and especially by the Sisters, who devote their lives to teaching you, to giving you a good example, to helping you in every way. They're very dedicated people, and I know that you realize it, and are obedient and helpful to them and appreciative of all that they do to help you become fine men and women and devoted Americans, and are very faithful to the practice of your religion. I know that a cardinal has many duties and many privileges, but there's one that I never forget, and that is that a cardinal has the right to give a holiday. So, with Sister Allen's permission, I ask that you be granted a holiday, and I promise Sister Allen, and all the other Sisters and teachers, that you will study harder the other days, so they won't write me any letters and say they didn't appreciate the holiday. So, please study hard and get me off the hook. Thank you very much. God bless you.

A CHAT WITH CARDINAL CUSHING
AT NEWTON CENTER

Sacred Heart Church in Newton Center, Massachusetts, is the only church in America which can boast that two of its priests have become cardinals — Cardinal Spellman and another famous American Cardinal, Richard Cushing. Cardinal Cushing was most pleased to come back to his old church and chat with Cardinal Spellman about their early days as priests here in Newton Center.

CARDINAL SPELLMAN. It's wonderful to be back in Newton Center.

CARDINAL CUSHING. It's fine to see you. Where do you come from now?

CARDINAL SPELLMAN. We came from the Cardinal Spellman High School in Brockton, where I expressed publicly my gratitude to Your Eminence for honoring me by having the high school named after me. And I'm very happy that we're associated, that the auditorium has your honored name.

CARDINAL CUSHING. That's right. So, we're both together down there, even as we were together up here.

CARDINAL SPELLMAN. Especially here in Newton Center.

CARDINAL SPELLMAN. I'm very glad to be back here. I saw the children filing out. I saw the playground which we've combined to purchase for their use. I saw some of the Sisters, and it really was a very poignant experience for me, because it's twenty-seven years since I left here.

CARDINAL CUSHING. It's very appropriate, Your Eminence, that this year happens to be the seventy-fifth anniversary of the parish.

CARDINAL SPELLMAN. Oh?

CARDINAL CUSHING. I came here in 1939. I was here five years. I succeeded Your Eminence.

CARDINAL SPELLMAN. I know. You not only succeeded, but you were very successful.

CARDINAL CUSHING. Well, I don't know how successful I was, because all the while I was still at the Propagation of the Faith; but when I came here, you had liquidated all the enormous debts on the projects around here.

CARDINAL SPELLMAN. Yes, well, I was happy that last Sunday to be able to say that the parish was out of debt. I was able to have the confirmation of the children. And so I was happy passing this fine parish, with its wonderful, wonderful people, over to Your Eminence, and I'm sure that, having had them as your parishioners, you appreciate them as much as I did.

CARDINAL CUSHING. Yes. They were a splendid flock — there's no doubt about that. And very devoted to the Church. And it's a parish from which a number of vocations have come.

CARDINAL SPELLMAN. Some of the girls who were here in my time in the school are now nuns and Sisters.

CARDINAL CUSHING. That's right.

CARDINAL SPELLMAN. And we have two priests from my time who were here. So, of course, that's the wonderful consolation that we have.

CARDINAL CUSHING. How long was Your Eminence here — four years?

CARDINAL SPELLMAN. Seven years.

CARDINAL CUSHING. Oh, is that so?

CARDINAL SPELLMAN. Yes, I came in 1932, and I left in 1939. If my mathematics is correct, I think it's seven.

CARDINAL CUSHING. And during all that time you had all the confirmations?

CARDINAL SPELLMAN. Yes.

CARDINAL CUSHING. Of the Archdiocese.

CARDINAL SPELLMAN. But I enjoyed that.

CARDINAL CUSHING. You're the only bishop they know around here, anyway. Half of them call me Cardinal Spellman.

CARDINAL SPELLMAN. Well, I'm complimented.

CARDINAL CUSHING. You certainly left your impress around here, Your Eminence, because they all speak of you — men like Harry Blake, who was in the other day, his wife is very sick. . . .

CARDINAL SPELLMAN. Yes, I know it.

CARDINAL CUSHING. And he was speaking of you.

CARDINAL SPELLMAN. Well, I took care of his mother when she was very sick.

CARDINAL CUSHING. Is that so?

CARDINAL SPELLMAN. On Parker Street. It's wonderful to go through these different places and see the houses where you visited the sick. And, of course, I had the parochial life here, and I could do what we all do — visit the sick and also teach the children.

CARDINAL CUSHING. And it's wonderful to have you here in this rectory, and it's wonderful to be with you, because we were both here, and we had the same curates, and they were good curates.

CARDINAL SPELLMAN. They were wonderful.

CARDINAL CUSHING. And all of them have passed on, you know. We outlasted them all. I don't know what the secret is — they were much younger than we were. Probably they were more pious than we were.

CARDINAL SPELLMAN. Well, probably we gave them a harder life. I would like to make a little visit to the church before I go.

CARDINAL CUSHING. I hope you have a very blessed, pleasant fiftieth anniversary.

AGUA NICARAGUA

9 — AÉREO

C$1.50 1959 — AÉREO

EUREKA S P CO

AGUA NICARAGUA

9 — AÉREO

C$1.50 1959 — AÉREO

EUREKA S P CO

AGUA NICARAGUA

59 — AÉREO

C$1.50 1959 — AÉREO

AGUA NICARAGUA

STAMPS

For years, stamps have been the Cardinal's greatest hobby. The Cardinal, when he is in the Whitman area, always visits Sister Fidelma, who is in charge of the Cardinal Spellman Philatelic Museum which houses his unusual collection. She has been in charge of the Cardinal's collection from the time he was at Newton Center; when a Mrs. Corey gave him money to use "for any purpose at all," he gave the building — the first and only building built expressly for the display of stamps — to Regis College in Weston, Massachusetts. It was given in honor of his mother's sister, Sister Philomena, who was a member of the convent of the Community of the Sisters of St. Joseph of Boston and had taught at this small girl's college in New England. Along with him on his visit to the museum are two of his young grandnieces.

SISTER FIDELMA *(to the nieces)*. These stamps show your granduncle when he was down in Nicaragua. The Government of Nicaragua issued them to honor His Eminence and to commemorate his visit in 1959 as Papal Legate at the Eucharistic Congress.

CARDINAL SPELLMAN. There is history on our stamps. They're wonderful things. They mirror the past and look forward to the future. They honor cultural attainments, industrial works, domestic, civil, and social life. And religion is deeply concerned with culture and in the disseminaton of exact historic knowledge.

SISTER FIDELMA. Yes, people can come here and study these commemorative stamps and read the story here. *(To the girls.)* For example, they will tell you about the

*Former President Dwight D. Eisenhower gives
Cardinal Spellman first space letter,
carried by Discoverer 17 in 1960, plus the
thousands of stamps amassed during his
eight years in the White House as a gift
for the stamp museum in this jubilee year.*

National Parks. Our collection was given to us by Mr. Lee three years ago, and the covers were autographed by Harold Ickes, former Secretary of the Interior. And over here are stamps autographed by Princess Grace of Monaco. And we have some on music, medicine, Old Testament stamps given your great-uncle by the Israeli Government. Also, the United Nations and stamps about it, with quotations from famous Americans like Susan B. Anthony, woman suffragette, and Clara Barton who founded the American Red Cross, and Booker T. Washington, and many more. Girls, do you know the stamps your great-uncle was responsible for?

GIRLS. No.

CARDINAL SPELLMAN. Well, there were two. One was the Al Smith stamp; it was a rare event to have a commemorative stamp for a man not President of the United States. Postmaster General Hannegan was kind enough to authorize that. And then also the "In God We Trust" stamps which President Eisenhower authorized. Everybody seemed to be against having that stamp, but President Eisenhower thought it would be a good thing. He didn't think it was controversial at all. It didn't seem to violate the Church and State separation condition. So he gave orders to have a stamp printed, saying "In God We Trust." And he invited me to be down in Washington when the first stamp was issued, and he gave me the first sheet which he signed.

SISTER FIDELMA. How did you begin saving stamps?

CARDINAL SPELLMAN. I lived in Rome, and I got a lot of foreign stamps; so I started collecting them and putting them in a book. And then as I grew older and came back to America, I continued the custom, and then, of course, if there is one way that you can become a philatelist instead of a "stamp collector," it's to become a cardinal first, because you get so many gifts. For example, when Monsignor Broderick went with me to South America, he used to visit the Postmaster General and say, "You know that the Cardinal has quite a stamp collection, but he's a little weak in Ecuador." Soon we had plenty of Ecuador stamps. That way I got a complete collection of many countries. In fact, the postmasters of both New Zealand and Australia gave me their entire collections. And that's why we have such a good collection for the museum.

FAMILY REUNION

And when the Cardinal returns to Whitman, he stays at the home of his sister, Mrs. Pegnam, and there's always a meeting of the Spellman clan. Nieces and grandnieces, nephews and grandnephews — all the children and grandchildren of his brothers and sisters. Mrs. Pegnam herself has twenty-eight grandchildren.

CARDINAL SPELLMAN. How are you?

MRS. PEGNAM. Just fine. I'm so glad to have you home. Come into the living room. Children, go into the living room. *(To the children.)* You can kiss Uncle Frank on the cheek — everyone else has.

CARDINAL SPELLMAN. Hello. How are you? What grade are you in?

CHILD. Third.

CARDINAL SPELLMAN. Are you doing well? Did you get any *A*'s?

CHILD. Yes.

CARDINAL SPELLMAN. Oh, good. I'm glad *somebody* did. Is this Julie?

JULIE. Yes.

CARDINAL SPELLMAN. Do you graduate this year?

JULIE. No, in three years. I'm a freshman now.

CARDINAL SPELLMAN. And what's your name?

IAN. Ian McCarthy.

CARDINAL SPELLMAN. And what grade are you in?

IAN. Second.

CARDINAL SPELLMAN. What's the name of the school?

IAN. Gurney.

CARDINAL SPELLMAN. Oh, Gurney. I went to Gurney School myself. Well, I hope some of you girls will grow up and become Sisters, so that we won't have such a shortage. Are you thinking of it at all?

CHILD. I don't want to.

CARDINAL SPELLMAN. What's your grade?

CHILD. I'm in the first.

CARDINAL SPELLMAN. Do you have a Sister teach you?

CHILD. Yeah.

CARDINAL SPELLMAN. What's the Sister's name?

CHILD. Sister Teresa.

CARDINAL SPELLMAN. What did you learn last week?

CHILD. Religion.

CARDINAL SPELLMAN. Religion? What kind of religion did you learn? Do you know who made the world yet?

CHILD. God.

CARDINAL SPELLMAN. Good. That's fine. And you go to the same school?

NIECE. No, she doesn't go to any.

CHILD. I go to kindergarten. I quit.

CARDINAL SPELLMAN. You quit kindergarten? Oh, that's a little premature.

NIECE. She's a dropout. We call her a dropout.

CARDINAL SPELLMAN. Why didn't you keep on going to school?

CHILD. I'm going next summer.

CARDINAL SPELLMAN. Next summer? That's better than going in the winter. Well, can you sing a song? How about the children who go to one school. Can they sing a song?

JULIE. How about some cheers from school — Spellman cheers.

CARDINAL SPELLMAN. Well, let's hear a cheer for Spellman. He needs it.

VOICES.

> Foundation with a Spellman
> Delegation when we fight with
> Determination we create a great sensation (repeat)
> T H U N D E R ! !

CARDINAL SPELLMAN. No lightning with it?

BROTHERS AND SISTERS

The Spellmans are a hearty stock. His father lived to be ninety-three, and his sisters and two brothers are still hale and healthy. They were all there for the reunion: Mrs. Pegnam, of course; his sister Helene, Mrs. Garrity, who also lives in Whitman. And his two brothers, Dr. Martin and Dr. John Spellman, who live in the Boston area. After the children went to bed, they had a chat.

DR. MARTIN. Someone just asked if I thought Whitman has changed in fifty years.

CARDINAL SPELLMAN. Well, I'm the only one that can talk about that. I'm the oldest.

DR. MARTIN. Well, go ahead. How do you think it has changed in fifty years?

CARDINAL SPELLMAN. For the better.

DR. MARTIN. Well, there are more people.

CARDINAL SPELLMAN. Yes, we now have twelve thousand.

DR. JOHN. At that time, there were about seventy-five hundred.

CARDINAL SPELLMAN. Well, that was ten years after I was born.

FRANCES *(interrupting)*. How did the family come to live here in the first place, Uncle Frank?

CARDINAL SPELLMAN. Because we were lucky.

DR. JOHN. Because we got out of the potato famine.

CARDINAL SPELLMAN. All of our grandparents came from Ireland — in the steerage — and they settled in Massachusetts when they landed in the United States. Then they came to Whitman.

DR. MARTIN. Well, I think the shoe business attracted Grandfather Spellman to Whitman. He started making shoes, at night, at home on Glenn Street. I think a lot of Irish immigrants landed in Boston, and they were a little crowded, and a good many of them went into the suburbs, and this was one of the suburban areas.

John

Marian

Martin

Helene

CARDINAL SPELLMAN. Well, our mother's parents came here, because they were settled in Plimpton, Massachusetts, and my Grandfather Conway had a yoke of oxen, and he had to cart the produce from East Whitman to Boston with the oxen. And the reason that they settled in Whitman was because my grandmother wanted to go to church, and there was no church at that time in the Plimpton area; and so she got my grandfather, her husband, to move to Whitman, where they bought a house. And they had a mortgage on it, and it took them ten years to pay the mortgage off at ten dollars a year. So, it was some house.

DR. MARTIN. Now it takes us twenty years to pay it.

CARDINAL SPELLMAN. And then, of course, they lived in East Whitman, and they brought up a family, and one of their daughters became a nun, Sister Philomena, and one of the other daughters became your mother, the mother of all of us. Yes. So that was the Conway part. The Spellmans, as you say, they started making shoes, boots, and they lived in Whitman, up on Glenn Street; and then they moved to Dover Street, and they mortgaged the house again — it was a different house — and put my father in the grocery business, which was lucky for you, Martin.

DR. MARTIN. Yes, I'm sure of that. It's been very helpful to me and all of us.

Mother

▲ *Helene*   ▼ *Martin*   ▲ *Marian*   ▼ *John*

A DAY WITH THE CARDINAL

What is an average day like for the Cardinal? His schedule remains full with little concession to his age. The hours of the day are continually filled with appointments, meetings, appearances. Travel is second nature to him, and one day he may be in Washington, the next in California, the next Albany. On just one day in New York, between the hours of nine and five, we followed him as he went to the Bronx for a funeral, blessed a new tropical-center research laboratory, was interviewed by the press, made a speech, visited with the sick, checked over his building programs, and conducted a Catholic Charities board meeting — sandwiching in a sizable amount of dictation and office work in the in-between minutes. But he never becomes too rushed for the people who gather wherever he goes. For them, his warm, easy smile is ready to put them at ease immediately. And for most of them who are Catholic, their feeling of good fortune to see the Cardinal becomes immediately apparent as they kneel, out of respect and devotion, to kiss his ring.

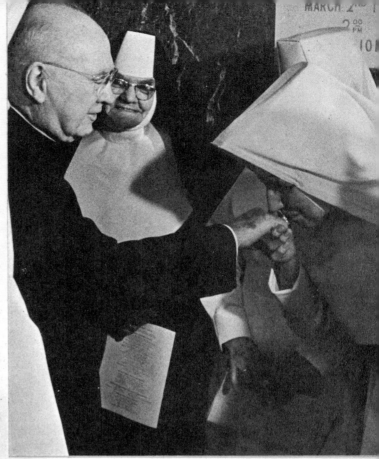

CAR RIDE

The Cardinal begins this busy day with his secretary Monsignor Patrick Ahern and Bishop Terence Cook. It was an unhappy last-minute addition to the schedule as they set off from Fiftieth Street to the Bronx for the funeral of the Cardinal's old classmate, the famous coach of the Fordham baseball team, Jack Coffey. In the car, they have a chance to chat.

CARDINAL SPELLMAN. We are on this large schedule. Nevertheless I wanted to go to Jack Coffey's funeral. He was really Mr. Fordham down through all the decades.

AHERN. I remember in 1961 the dinner when he received the medal from Fordham for fifty years.

CARDINAL SPELLMAN. Fifty years is a long time.

BISHOP COOK. Was that the first time you were ever in New York — when you came down to Fordham?

CARDINAL SPELLMAN. Oh, no. I had relatives in New York. They lived down on the lower East Side — 88 Madison Street. Then there was another relative who lived at 49 West 46 Street. Without them, I probably wouldn't have gone to Fordham. Actually it was my mother's idea. She thought that I knew all about Massachusetts and had done enough around home. She thought that it would be good to get away from Massachusetts. Not because we didn't like Massachusetts — we loved it — but she thought that it would be well if I knew some other place beside it. And I was lucky to be born as early as I was, because now when you go to college you have to go through so many tests that I'm sure I wouldn't have passed. I was glad that all I had to do was have a high-school diploma, and I was admitted to Fordham. That was back in 1907. And what followed were four very, very happy years, and the friends I met at Fordham

87

College photo, Fordham

— my classmates — have remained friends ever since. Those that are still alive. But we're dying off rather rapidly; there aren't many of us left from the Class of 1911.

AHERN. How many were in the class originally?

CARDINAL SPELLMAN. Forty-three.

AHERN. And how many are left?

CARDINAL SPELLMAN. Well, I don't know whether I'm left or not. But only a few.

AHERN. It's nice that Monsignor Joe McCaffrey is going to be able to say the Mass for Jack today.

CARDINAL SPELLMAN. Yes, he was the president of our class. I think the vice-president is already dead. I don't know who he was now. But that's why I want to go to the funeral, because you only have one chance at a funeral.

BISHOP COOK. Jack Coffey used to say that you were a great baseball player.

CARDINAL SPELLMAN. Well, Jack was a little optimistic. As I told Monsignor Ahern, the way to become a ballplayer is to become a cardinal first!

AHERN. Not a St. Louis Cardinal, Your Eminence.

CARDINAL SPELLMAN. No, I'm no Joe Medwick or Frankie Frisch.

BISHOP COOK. What do you look back upon most fondly at Fordham?

CARDINAL SPELLMAN. The friends I had there. The friends I made. It was a wonderful group of men.

AHERN. And it was also a great preparation for your coming to New York a second time, Your Eminence. It was about —

CARDINAL SPELLMAN. Yes, twenty-seven years ago.

AHERN. Of course, that was a great break for us.

CARDINAL SPELLMAN. Thank you. You're just saying that. But I treasure the memory of my friends and acquaintances more than I do my recollections of Greek and Latin. They've done me more good, the friends, than the Greek and Latin did. Well, the Latin was a little help, especially in the Ecumenical Council.

Graduating Class, 1911, Fordham

POETRY

AHERN. You know, besides almost being a baseball star at Fordham —

CARDINAL SPELLMAN. You're so charitable.

AHERN. — were you involved in any other student activities? Debating? I know you wrote some poetry once.

CARDINAL SPELLMAN. Yes, my poetry days are over, too.

AHERN. Have you read any of it recently?

CARDINAL SPELLMAN. Read any poetry recently?

AHERN. No. Any of the poetry you wrote in Fordham.

CARDINAL SPELLMAN. No.

AHERN. I was wondering how they stood up.

CARDINAL SPELLMAN. Well, I don't think they stand up very well. I had two verses — not poems; you can't say poems unless you're a poet — in the November 1908 issue of the *Fordham Monthly,* which was the first year that we were taught poetry.

AHERN. But you won a number of prizes for your poems.

BISHOP COOK. Didn't you win a trip to Washington?

CARDINAL SPELLMAN. That wasn't Fordham. That was up in Whitman. Whitman High. And I won five dollars. The Whitman's Women's Club put up a prize — to the senior at Whitman High School who wrote the essay on the students' trip to Washington that they thought was the best. So, I had a couple of anecdotes in there that a couple of the other students didn't have, and I was lucky.

AHERN. And there's a rumor around that you were in the Glee Club at Fordham; they say it's exaggerated.

CARDINAL SPELLMAN. I was as good in the Glee Club as I was on the baseball diamond — that is, no good! Just because you fellows are singers . . .

In the latter part of October
   When Jack Frost is beginning to bite,
May be seen in the woods of New England,
   A gleeful and jolly sight.

The carefree laughter of children
   Is borne on the autumn breeze,
With a ring that comes forth when the axhead
   Pierces one of the giant trees.

When their school day duties are over,
   They hastily wend their way
Toward the place where the shagbark lures them,
   In the woods where the chipmunks play . . . .

Oh happy hours of my childhood!
   Alas! All too quickly sped;
But remembrance will cling to me always,
   Till I enter the ranks of the dead.

The Whitman High School graduating class tours Washington, D.C., in 1907. Frank Spellman is the lad in the center with his leg swung over the side of the horse-drawn omnibus.

BLESSING THE LABORATORY

The reporters and television men were ready to ask questions and take pictures when the Cardinal arrived at St. Clare's Hospital to bless the new Tropical Disease Research Center laboratory. Every public move of the Cardinal is eagerly reported by the press. He is always ready with a quick answer.

LADY REPORTER. Your Eminence, I wonder if you could explain the import and also the details of the new regulations on fast days.

CARDINAL SPELLMAN. They were explained by the Holy Father. I'm not going to repeat his explanation.

LADY REPORTER. Was this a project that was widely discussed at the Council?

CARDINAL SPELLMAN. No.

LADY REPORTER. Did it come as a surprise to you?

CARDINAL SPELLMAN. Nothing comes as a surprise to me.

In the laboratory, the Cardinal begins the blessing.

CARDINAL SPELLMAN. O Lord, bless our works and accompany them to completion, that our every prayer and work may ever begin with You and through You be accomplished. O God, to whom every heart opens, every mind speaks, and nothing remains hidden, change our innermost thoughts by an infusion of the Holy Spirit that worthily and well we may perform this blessing and thereby obtain for Your servants the welfare they seek. O God, who wondrously freed man and still more wondrously have transformed him by Your Grace, Who also heals with manifold remedies the infirmities that beset human frailties, we pour forth and beseech Your blessing upon this Tropical Disease Research Center. May those who will be treated here find in You a fatherly protector and a loving physician of both body and soul. We ask this for Jesus Christ Your son, our Lord, Who lives and reigns with You in union with the Holy Spirit of God forever. Sprinkle me with hyssop, O Lord, and I shall be clean; wash me, and I shall be whiter than snow. . . .

After the blessing, the reporters asked the Cardinal to pose looking through a microscope. With his usual spirit of fun, he agreed.

"THE CARDINAL WILL SAY A FEW WORDS"

Wherever the Cardinal goes, he is always asked to say a few words. During the ride back from the funeral, Monsignor Ahern broached the subject.

AHERN. After the blessing itself, Your Eminence, there will be a little civic ceremony, and then Congressman Fogarty is going to speak and a few others, and then —

CARDINAL SPELLMAN. He's always good. He's a great speaker and a great man, and he's done an awful lot for hospital improvement.

AHERN. Yes, and then maybe —

CARDINAL SPELLMAN. I'm very happy he's from New England.

AHERN. Maybe at the end, you'd say a few words informally, Your Eminence.

BISHOP COOK. I thought you'd have a speech for the Cardinal. Help him out, you know.

CARDINAL SPELLMAN (joking). I thought you'd write out something for me.

AHERN. You know, Monsignor Quinn always says, "Your Eminence, you're better when you're not prepared."

CARDINAL SPELLMAN. Yes, but that isn't quite the right quotation: "You're better when you don't know what you're talking about."

On the dais, listening to the speakers.

The Cardinal's speech was a great success.

CARDINAL SPELLMAN *(speaking at the dedication).* You can make a speech for me, Sister, if you want to, because as usual I'm not prepared. But I am prepared to express gratitude to those who have participated in the program today, especially to Congressman Fogarty and to Commissioner Yerby for their presence. It is a great honor to St. Clare's and a great pleasure for me to hear them. Congressman Fogarty has embarrassed me a little bit talking about thirteen million and nine million and millions scattered all over the lot, because I was told by Dr. Kale what we could do for ninety thousand dollars. I said, "Well, that's wonderful. I never got so much for so little." . . . So we got off to a good start with this ninety thousand dollars, and Congressman Fogarty can multiply it into several million down in Congress, and Sister John Kevin I am sure will supervise the expenditure by Dr. Kale. So, I think we're on safe ground. Naturally, it's a great joy for me to be here. I had a bout with tropical diseases myself. I'd made the mistake of telling the doctor when I was sick that I'd been in South America. So, he decided he'd make a very thorough investigation, and he tried everything on me, but he found out I didn't have any tropical diseases. But anyway I'm glad to have contributed so much to medical progress. . . .

After the speech, the Cardinal was presented with a bouquet of roses.

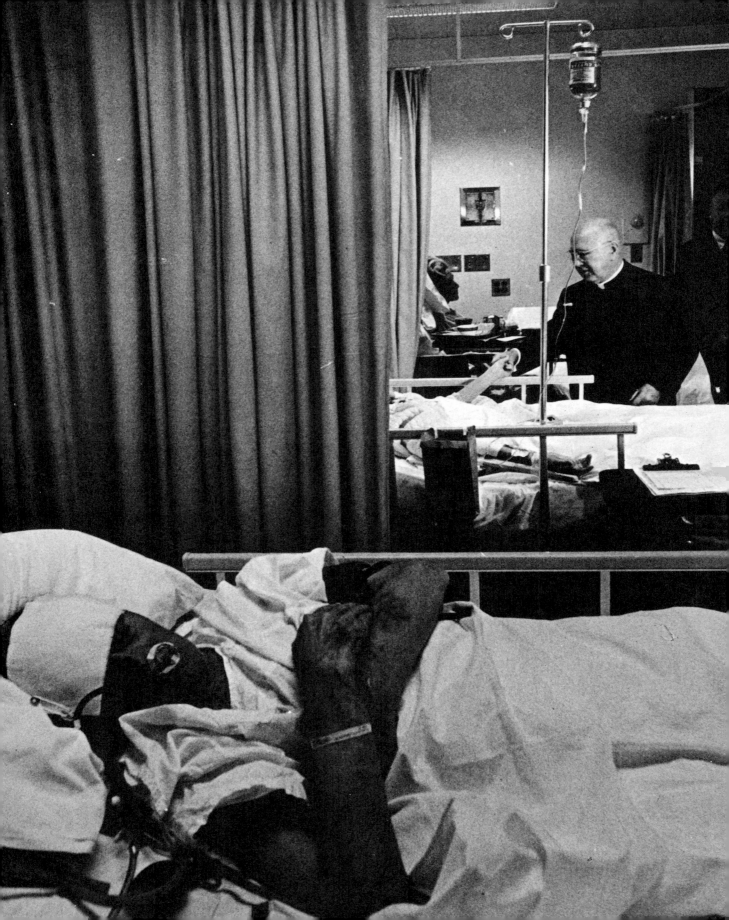

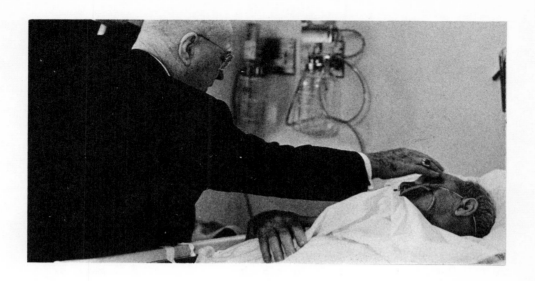

VISITING THE SICK

The Tropical Disease Center is just one of the research programs made possible by grants from the Cardinal. Another program is concerned with Hodgkins' disease, and another for experimentally induced cancer and its cure. And there are always more and more hospitals in his plans — excellent hospitals such as St. Vincent's, St. Francis, Misericordia — to provide the best in medical care for the sick. But for the spirit of the patients, nothing is better than a visit from the Cardinal himself. Sunday afternoons, whenever there is time, the Cardinal visits them, bringing comfort even to the most gravely ill with a blessing and a touch of the hands.

MRS. REYES

But there is one patient that the Cardinal never forgets at St. Clare's — Mrs. Reyes. She was badly burned while praying in St. Patrick's Cathedral in April, 1965. The Cardinal, Bishop Cook, and Monsignor Ahern spoke of her on the way to visit her.

CARDINAL SPELLMAN. Mrs. Reyes was praying very devoutly at the altar rail at St. Patrick's Cathedral, and some maniac came in and threw a Molotov cocktail. I don't know at whom it was aimed, but it hit her and burned her very badly. She's been in the hospital most of the time since then. But she's very heroic about it, very resigned, and has even prayed for the person who threw the bomb. Thank God, nobody was killed. The cathedral was damaged, but that's insignificant compared to what happened to Mrs. Reyes. In my estimation, she really is qualified to be a heroine, because she took her misfortune in such a resigned manner.

AHERN. Remember, we went over the night it happened, Your Eminence. You had a dinner at the Waldorf, and Bishop Cook and Monsignor Kenney — Lord have mercy on him — and I, got you, and we went over to the hospital about half past ten, and Mrs. Reyes was blaming herself; she said, "It's really my own fault. It's on account of vanity that it happened, because I went to buy a new hat, and I don't really need a new hat. I'm just too fond of them. Otherwise, I wouldn't have been there."

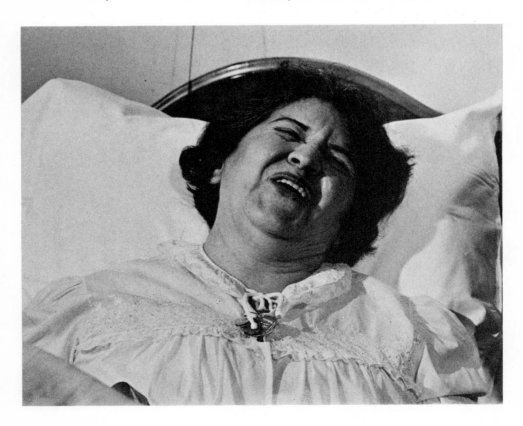

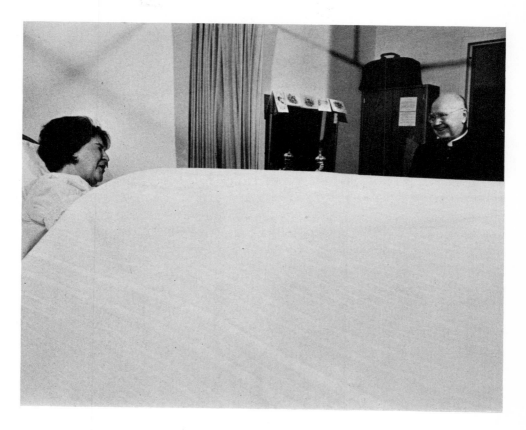

Bishop Cook. So, she had the new hat.

Ahern. Yes, the new hat was destroyed in the accident.

Bishop Cook. Everything was just charcoaled — the railing of the sanctuary . . .

Ahern. I don't know how many skin grafts she had, but the other day I got a card from her, and she said, "My Valentine's present was another skin graft." She had it on Valentine's Day, and she said, "I hope that's the last." I think it is, the final one. And she should get out, Your Eminence, in a few weeks. And then it's hoped that she may stay in one of our other homes like the Josephine Baird Home up on Fifty-fifth Street for a while to take the whirlpool treatments. Then she'll be able to go home.

Cardinal Spellman. Well, whatever we can do for her we want to do, because she has given a great example of resignation, of fortitude, and also of religion.

Ahern. Yes, she's most grateful for everything. The thing, I think, that touched her most was when you got the autographed picture of our Holy Father, while you were over at the last Council session, and sent it. She was really moved by that.

Bishop Cook. Yes. And she certainly has been encouraged by all the visits that you've made to her over these months.

A GIFT OF ROSES

As soon as the Cardinal walked into her room with a huge bouquet of roses, Mrs. Reyes was full of smiles.

CARDINAL SPELLMAN. Hello, Mrs. Reyes. How are you?

MRS. REYES. Oh, Your Eminence, it's so good of you to come. Thank you for your kindness in coming.

The Cardinal gives Mrs. Reyes the bouquet of roses, which had been presented to him after his speech in the auditorium.

MRS. REYES. Oh, thank you. Thank you very much. God bless you.

CARDINAL SPELLMAN. I don't want to be here under false colors. I didn't go out and buy these roses. But they gave them to me. These didn't cost me anything.

MRS. REYES. Oh?

CARDINAL SPELLMAN. I want to make a confession. I try to get as much work out of flowers as I can. I gave them to Sister John Kevin first. Then she gave them back to me. And now you're getting them — but don't you give them away.

MRS. REYES. I won't give them to anybody. I appreciate very much your kindness to me.

CARDINAL SPELLMAN. Well, it's the least I could do. You've the spirit of a Joan of Arc. You've been so brave during all this trouble.

MRS. REYES (*kissing the Cardinal's ring*). Oh, thank you.

CARDINAL SPELLMAN. You'll soon be at the Josephine Baird Home. I'll be able to see you there.

MRS. REYES. Oh, thank you.

CARDINAL SPELLMAN. God bless you. (*He blesses her.*) Well, it's wonderful to see you. And be sure and don't give the flowers away now.

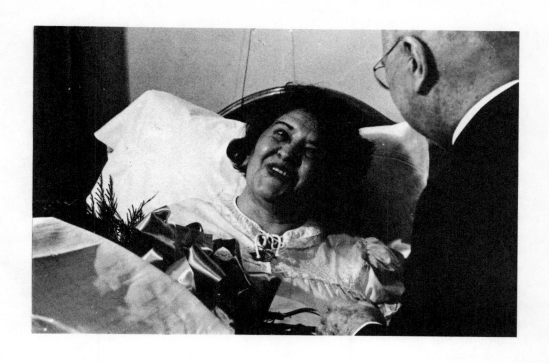

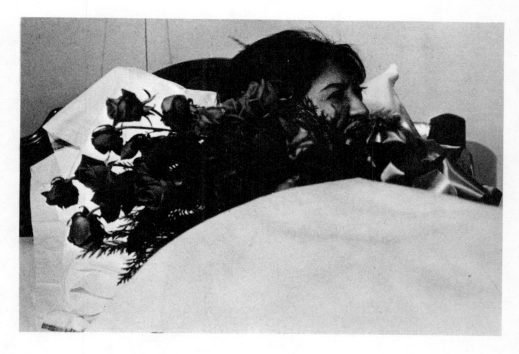

DICTATION

During spare minutes of the day, and often late into the night, the Cardinal dictates an almost endless outpouring of words, filling one dictation cylinder after another with letters, memorandums, speeches, sermons, reports. He was the first cardinal to fly a plane, the first cardinal to have a pilot's license, and the first cardinal to use a dictating machine. From one wartime trip alone, he corresponded with the families of over fourteen thousand servicemen.

CARDINAL SPELLMAN DICTATES A LETTER

Dear Bishop O'Sullivan:

I have your note, and I wish to express my gratitude to you for your kindness in serving as Chaplain Delegate for the Thirteenth Area of the United States, including the Alaskan Command, the Alaskan Air Command, and the Alaskan Sea Frontier in the United States Army of Alaska.

I am most appreciative of all that you have done during these nineteen years that you have served the American forces in these areas. I shall follow your suggestion and appoint someone to relieve you of your duties, someone from the Diocese of Anchorage.

I will assume that the most logical appointment would be Archbishop Ryan, who has himself served with the Marines during the recent hostilities.

Once more, thank you for your kindnesses and with best wishes, I am very sincerely yours in Christ. . . .

Send this correspondence, and write a note to Archbishop Ryan, in which he is appointed the Chaplain Delegate of the Thirteenth Area, including the Alaskan Command, the Alaskan Air Command, and the Alaskan Sea Frontier in the United States Army of Alaska.

I am sending herewith a pagella of the facilities — P-A-G-E-L-L-A — for your use. With kind regards and best wishes, I am very sincerely yours in Christ.

And then the correspondence can go to the Military Ordinariat.

BUILDING PROGRAMS

The Cardinal's building program has been far-reaching from the first. The Cardinal Hayes High School, which was built when he first came to New York, was the key project, costing three million dollars. And with its success, many, many more were to follow — seminaries, schools, hospitals — always with the best and most up-to-date facilities. Monsignor Leonard Hunt, in charge of the program, reviewed the boundaries of the Archdiocese on the map in the third floor of the Chancery and showed some pictures of the one hundred and eleven million dollars worth of building which have just been finished or are under construction.

MONSIGNOR HUNT. The Archdiocese of New York covers 4,717 square miles. Three of the boroughs of New York City are part of the diocese — Staten Island, Manhattan, and the Bronx. And then there are seven other counties lining the Hudson River, from Westchester County to Dutchess and Ulster Counties. We go to the northern line of Ulster County. And we go on our east-west dimension from the Connecticut border to the Delaware River. This is an extremely difficult dimension to travel, and it makes it very difficult for us, because the roads mostly are in a north-south direction, rather than east-west.

CARDINAL SPELLMAN. Are you suggesting another diocese? Or otherwise, we might be able to have a helicopter to cover it?

MONSIGNOR HUNT. It includes a number of large cities — Yonkers, White Plains, New Rochelle, Newburgh, Poughkeepsie, Beacon, and Kingston — along with Middletown and some of the others. A great deal of the area is still rural, quite a difference from Manhattan and the Bronx. In fact, it's mostly rural from the northern Rockland County line straight up, with the exception of Poughkeepsie along the Hudson River. The Orange County area is very rolling country and a fine dairy area. Recently there have been some changes. We are discovering that, with the Thruway and the Tappan Zee Bridge, people are working in White Plains and coming across the Tappan Zee Bridge and up the Thruway, and are living in the southern part of Orange County. The urbification in that area is greater than it's ever been. So, we're now in the process of developing schools in these areas because of the influx of new population. Here are some of the schools that we have constructed in the not-so-distant past. This school here is in Hartsdale. It's the Maria Regina High School. And the school over the other side is Monsignor Farrell High School in Staten Island.

Some of the other work that we've done that we're particularly proud of is the restoration of the original church in State Street down in the Wall Street district which we've dedicated to Mother Seton. She actually lived in a tenement that was on the site of the new shrine here. And we have in this building a very fine example of the Federalist period of architecture. And we have tried to conform as much as possible with the existing architecture. This is a definite landmark in old New York.

▲ *Monsignor Farrell High School.*   ▼ *Mother Seaton Restoration.*

The Cardinal is a superb administrator, the director of over 150 boards, in charge of 403 parishes, a life member of the NAACP, even on the Board of the New York Public Library. In the Gold Room of the Chancery, each month, the Cardinal presides over the most important Catholic Charities Board of Directors meetings. Founded forty-seven years ago, Catholic Charities, through a network of 201 agencies, helps those who need it. Last year, for example 23,657 families were helped and 16,359 children were cared for through Catholic Charities. Total expenditures for 1965 alone were $5,967,940.82.

The meetings always begin with a prayer.

CARDINAL SPELLMAN. Hail, Mary, full of grace, the Lord is with thee. Blessed are thou among women, and blessed is the fruit of thy womb, Jesus.

BOARD MEMBERS. Holy Mary, mother of God, pray for us sinners now and at the hour of our death. Amen.

CARDINAL SPELLMAN. Queen of peace, pray for us. In the name of the Father and of the Son and of the Holy Spirit. Amen.

The members of the board include John A. Coleman, Victor Siminsky, Frank Folsom, John Burke, Jr. — some of the most influential, wealthy, and intelligent men in America. And the board meetings are all very democratic. The Cardinal's manner is informal. Everyone speaks his mind, every now and then disagreeing with the Cardinal. But the final decision is his. It's his yes or no that counts.

"HOW DOES IT FEEL TO BE SEVENTY-SEVEN?"

AHERN. How does it feel to be seventy-seven, Your Eminence?

CARDINAL SPELLMAN. Being alive is kind of a miraculous thing.

AHERN. Wasn't it Maurice Chevalier, Your Eminence, who, when they said, "How does it feel to be seventy-five?" answered, "Wonderful — when I consider the alternative!"

CARDINAL SPELLMAN. Of course, there are two alternatives. (Pause.) Well, it certainly gives you a strong reason for meditating on the final disposition of your body and soul.

AHERN. Well, it's nice to have seventy-seven years, Your Eminence.

CARDINAL SPELLMAN. Yes, I'm glad I've had them.

BISHOP COOK. Well, we are too.

AHERN. I'm not sure I wouldn't rather have them in front of me, though.

CARDINAL SPELLMAN. No, I'm satisfied.

THE PRIVATE CHAPEL

The days are full. But they all begin in the same way. For like all priests of the Roman Catholic Church the world over, each and every day for the past fifty years, the Cardinal has proclaimed his faith with a Mass to celebrate the glory of God. For most of the past twenty-seven years, this Mass has been said in his private chapel on the third floor of his residence directly above his sitting room on Madison Avenue.

Monsignor Ahern serves him at Mass, helping him into the alb, the robe of white
linen which covers the body, symbolizing light, joy, and purity.

My yoke is sweet and My burden light. . . .
Grant that I may so carry it as to merit thy grace.

At Christmas time, our soldiers have the inspiration of the Cardinal himself to say Mass for them on the battlefront. Korea, the South Pole, Alaska, Berlin, Tokyo, Malta, Iwo Jima, Vietnam — where hasn't he been? For twenty-five years, the Cardinal made his parish the world of the lonely American soldier sent far from home; and yet, this man once was told he was temperamentally unfit for the Navy. He would not accept that decision. Instead, he became the most famous military vicar of the world. What is it in this man that enabled him to do this? Irish determination? Yankee stubbornness? Or was it a human spirit . . . and faith . . . which perhaps best typifies him as a man — strong, vibrant, and eternally young.

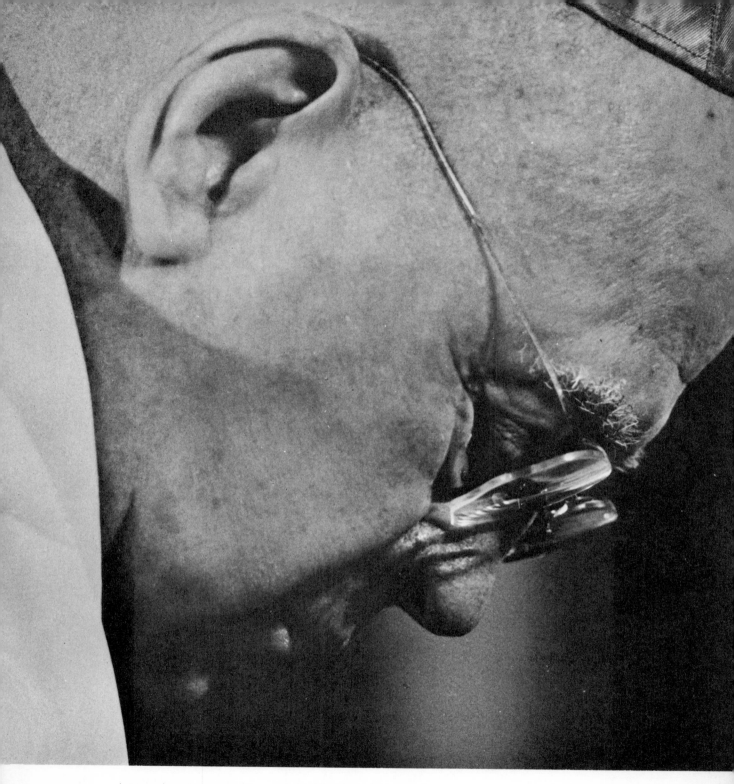

Eternally young, as he repeats the words of the Mass:
I will go to the altar of God,
To God who gives joy to my youth.